I Like To Eat Trea[ts]

Written by B. Annye Rothenberg, Ph.D.
Child/Parent Psychologist

Illustrated by David T. Wenzel

REDWOOD CITY, CALIFORNIA

DEDICATION

For all parents who strive tirelessly to encourage their children to eat enough healthy food and to enjoy being active – both being essential for a quality life.

And for my son, Bret, *who was wonderful as a boy and is "the best" as a man (and now he always eats his fruit and … mostly … eats his vegetables)!* —B.A.R.

Text copyright © 2010 by B. Annye Rothenberg

Illustrations copyright © 2010 by David T. Wenzel

Library of Congress Cataloging-in-Publication Data

Rothenberg, B. Annye, 1940-
 I like to eat treats / written by B. Annye Rothenberg ; illustrated by David T. Wenzel.
   p. cm.
 ISBN 978-0-9790420-2-7 (pbk.)
 1. Children--Nutrition. 2. Children--Nutrition--Juvenile literature. I. Wenzel, David, 1950- II. Title.
 RJ206.R7286 2010
 613.2083--dc22

                        2009015058

Printed in China.   First printing January, 2010
10 9 8 7 6 5 4 3 2 1

Children's book in collaboration with
SuAnn and Kevin Kiser
Palo Alto, California

Parents' manual edited by
Caroline Grannan
San Francisco, California

Book design by
Cathleen O'Brien
San Francisco, California

REDWOOD CITY, CALIFORNIA

Published by
PERFECTING PARENTING PRESS
www.PerfectingParentingPress.com

To parents and parenting guidance professionals:

• WHAT'S IN THIS BOOK
FOR CHILDREN AND FOR PARENTS •

This third book in a series focuses on a **child-rearing goal with clear lifelong benefits: teaching young children what foods keep them healthy and strong.** This two-part book begins with a humorous story educating three- to six-year-olds about the difference between healthy and treat* foods, as well as what foods they need each day and why. The second part is a comprehensive parent guidance section that helps you learn more about nutrition for the family. **Together, these two parts help parents and young children learn what's important about food and exercise.**

Jack, the young child in the children's story, loves to eat treats. His parents are teaching him why it's not good for his body to have too many treat foods. Jack learns about quality food by shopping, cooking, and talking with his parents as they prepare a dinner for friends. He begins to see what role treats or "splurges" can play in his daily diet. As you read this book, ask your child if what happens in the story sounds like something that happens in your home. "What do Mommy and Daddy say when you want a lot of treats? Why? What do you think about having treats? Did you like what Jack said? Was he funny?" Your child may ask some difficult questions about nutrition and about exercise. The parent guidance section will give you most of the answers. Learning about nutrition requires lots of repetition, experience, and time before your child will grasp what it's truly about.

The parenting section will clear up confusion about what children need to eat and how to make sure that parents' expectations are reasonable. The manual addresses all the issues that parents struggle with about their children's eating, such as how much and what kids should be expected to eat; how to teach children acceptable eating behavior and get them to stay at the table; handling refusals to eat certain foods such as vegetables; and what to do about desserts. **It also discusses other common preschool and kindergarten-age eating problems, including picky eaters, undereaters, and overeaters, and gives parents important insight and practical advice.** Section One teaches all about realistic nutrition and encouraging more exercise. Section Two helps parents guide eating behavior. Section Three deals with preventing and handling picky eating and Section Four with overeating. Last, Section Five helps you monitor your children's eating and recommends additional resources. This parenting section includes case studies – examples from families of preschoolers and kindergartners – and **concludes with a summary of practical guidelines**.

— *Annye Rothenberg, Ph.D., Child/Parent Psychologist, in consultation with pediatric dietitians*

*In this book, **treats** mean foods that have great taste appeal (sweet, salty, high in fat) but aren't quality nutrition and should be limited.

One day, I went to the supermarket with Mommy and Daddy. I love the supermarket! We were there to buy food to make a special dinner for my friend Madeline and her parents.

"Can I get a donut?" I asked.

"Not now, Jack," said Daddy. "We're going to have a treat later, and we can only have one treat a day."

"But I need a donut now," I said. "My tummy says so."

"Honey," said Mommy, "it's time you learned something very important about treats like candy, potato chips, French fries, cake ..."

"And donuts?" I asked.

"And donuts," said Mommy. "The problem with treats, Jack, is that they aren't made of enough healthy things. They fill up your tummy, and don't leave enough room for foods that help you grow and be strong like Daddy and me."

"But I like to eat treats," I said.

"Lots of people do," said Daddy. "That's because treats taste very sweet or salty, which makes you want to eat too much of them."

"Is that why there's a rule about how many treats I can have?" I asked.

"Exactly," said Daddy. "Eating too many treats means you're not having enough of the food you need to eat."

"What food do I need to eat?" I asked.

"There are lots of foods that are healthy for you to eat, Jack," said Mommy. "Most of what you eat every day should be healthy foods."

"Healthy foods taste delicious too, Pumpkin," said Daddy, "but only if your body doesn't get used to too many treats."

"But how come other people in the store are buying a lot of treats?" I asked.

"Not every family has learned the rules about treats yet, Jack," said Mommy, "but more people are learning these rules every day."

"Are we going to have healthy foods when Madeline comes over for dinner?" I asked. "I want her to know what the best foods for her body are, too."

"We sure are," said Mommy. "We'll have a healthy dinner and a treat for dessert."

Daddy picked out a package of chicken. "Chicken is a healthy food because it has a lot of protein to help you grow strong and tall," he said.

"Like an elephant!" I said.

Daddy laughed and said, "That's right. And milk has protein and calcium too, so we'll have some with dinner."

"I know about milk," I said. "It makes my teeth and bones strong. Then I can chew through anything. Just like a beaver." I showed them my front teeth.

Mommy smiled and said, "Jack, you're so funny!"

"We should also drink water with our dinner," said Daddy. "It's good to drink a lot of water every day."

"Like a camel!" I said.

10

"We should have rice with our chicken," said Daddy. "Rice has carbohydrates that give us energy. When you have a lot of energy, you can play for a long time."

Daddy lifted me up so I could choose a package of rice.

"Let's have broccoli and a salad tonight," said Mommy. "I'll get the lettuce. Daddy can get the broccoli. Jack, see if you can find three carrots and two tomatoes to put in the salad."

"OK," I said. "We're getting a lot of vegetables."

"We sure are," said Daddy. "Vegetables have vitamins and minerals. So do fruits. When you eat fruits and vegetables, you don't get sick as often."

"Do they make my 'owies' get better?" I asked.

"Yes," said Mommy, "and some fruits and vegetables even help us see better in the dark."

"Like an owl!" I said.

"Just like an owl," said Daddy. "You sure are smart."

"We need some salad dressing too," said Mommy. "Salad dressing and some other foods have fat in them. They give extra flavor to our food and even help us feel full longer. But we only need a little of them."

"Now that we have a lot of healthy food," I said, "what treat are we going to get for dessert?"

"Let's see what they have in the bakery," said Mommy.

"Can we get apple pie?" I asked. "It tastes yummy and it has fruit in it too."

"Good idea, Jack," said Daddy.

In the check-out line, we used
our own cloth bags so we could
help the planet be healthy too.

When we got home, I washed my hands so I could help cook our special dinner.

"You can put the spices on the chicken," Daddy said.

"OK!" I said. I sprinkled some on — not too much — so the chicken would taste really delicious! Daddy put the chicken in the oven. Then he made the rice, while Mommy cooked the broccoli.

I tore the lettuce into little pieces. Then Mommy sliced tomatoes and grated carrots.

Soon everything was ready.

The doorbell rang. It was Madeline and her mommy and daddy. Madeline and I played while our mommies and daddies talked.

"We went shopping today to buy everything for dinner," I said. "Mommy and Daddy told me about healthy foods and treat foods. We're going to have a delicious dinner that's healthy."

"My mommy and daddy like healthy foods too," said Madeline. "But I'm not sure if I do. What are we having for dinner?"

"We're having chicken, rice, broccoli, and salad with dressing," I said. "Those are healthy foods that will help us grow tall like a giraffe and strong like a lion."

Madeline stood on her tiptoes and stretched her neck, and I roared like a lion.

"That was fun," Madeline said. "Are we having bananas for dessert? Then we could be monkeys."

"No," I said. "After we eat our healthy dinner, we get to have apple pie for dessert."

"I love apple pie!" said Madeline. "I'll eat everything on my plate!"

"Me too," I said. "Like a big hungry bear!"

Then we were both bears until
Mommy called us to eat.

"Dinner is delicious," said Madeline.
"I really like healthy foods."

"Me, too," I said. "I feel stronger and taller already."

Later, after Madeline and her parents went home, I said, "I know all about food now, and I just made up a poem."

"A poem!" said Mommy. "Wow!"

"We want to hear it, Jack," said Daddy.

I took a deep breath and began.

"I want lots of healthy foods in my tummy.

Then I can have one treat each day that is yummy."

We all laughed together ... and that was the best treat of all.

A GUIDANCE SECTION FOR PARENTS

• INTRODUCTION •

Parents want to teach their children to take good care of their bodies for life. To do this, parents need to learn more about preschoolers' and kindergartners' nutrition **and** need to practice better eating and lifestyle habits themselves. While we know how important food and exercise are for lifelong health, many factors work against successfully modeling positive habits for our children. Busy families have difficulty finding time to prepare nutritious meals and eat together, or to squeeze in family exercise like taking walks, bicycling, or kicking soccer balls. It's too easy to drive children everywhere, get take-out food, and let them have too much time with TV, electronic toys, and computers. This parents' manual will help you adopt healthier priorities for your family, with an emphasis on nutrition.

Many issues can develop around eating, sometimes involving parents' expectations. This first case study demonstrates a problem in which parents whose older child is a "good eater" struggle to understand why their younger son eats so little.

CASE STUDY: A DIFFERENT APPETITE

Sandra and David's two children showed very different eating patterns. Ben, now six years old, had always eaten a wide variety of foods. He had a good appetite and liked healthy food. He was growing well and had good energy. But food was a struggle with four-year-old Michael. He ate far less than Ben had at that age. Sandra and David also felt that Michael had less energy and stamina than his older brother. They were tempted to give Michael whatever he wanted to eat, just to give him enough calories. But they were concerned about treat foods becoming his dietary staple.

Tensions arose at meals and snack times. Michael's parents felt they were frequently pressuring him to eat. They had hoped that as he got older, they would be able to persuade him to try eating more variety and more calories. But Michael continued to have little interest in food. He ate slowly, and his parents insisted that he eat enough, so he was usually still at the table long after the rest of the family had finished. Sandra and David felt they were failing him. The frustration over Michael's eating was spilling over into other issues – they found themselves impatient with him while he was getting dressed, bathed, etc. Their annoyance seemed to cause Michael to become increasingly oppositional.

Michael's parents discussed his eating habits with their pediatrician and several close relatives. They realized that Michael's body type was similar to that of David's dad, a slender and short man who had always been a light eater. They began to understand that Michael might simply need much less food than his taller, more energetic brother to provide what he needed for his more moderate activity level. Michael's pediatrician helped them adjust their expectations and offer him smaller portions. Sandra and David began to see Michael as an individual with his own needs and body type. These new expectations enabled him to become more comfortable with food and feel accepted and valued for his differences and uniqueness. As his parents' frustrations decreased, Michael became generally more cooperative.

• SECTION ONE •
SMALL TUMMIES NEED BIG NUTRITION

Young children are delightful, fun-loving, and fascinating. Preschoolers are also challenging because they think quite differently from their parents and can quickly become oppositional, illogical, and rigid. Yet they are eager to learn. Kindergartners are usually easier to reason with. **Parents want their young children to begin to learn important lifelong habits.** That's why we teach them to take regular baths, wear clean clothes, pick up their toys, be polite, have enough sleep, and so on. **And that's why this book focuses on food and exercise.**

LET'S START WITH EXERCISE

Children should be encouraged to engage in physical activity adding up to at least an hour a day, in addition to the usual running, jumping, and climbing that young children naturally do. Some children get that hour on their own, but many don't. **Parents** with less-active children **need to find ways to make exercising a shared – and fun – family activity** (turning on music and dancing, walking, biking, kicking a soccer ball or playing other sports, going to the beach, gardening). When a child's food intake matches her[1] activity pattern, the child is likely to maintain normal weight for her height and body type. It pays to teach your child the habit of daily physical activity. It's much easier for anyone to continue exercising when it has always been a daily habit – like brushing her teeth – than to force herself to adopt the habit as an adult.

[1] *To avoid the awkward use of "he or she," the sections in this book will alternate between both.*

TEACHING YOUNG CHILDREN ABOUT HEALTHY EATING

As parents, we want our children to be accustomed to healthy eating from the earliest possible age so good nutrition will be a lifelong habit.

Young children are ready to begin to learn about nutrition ("healthy food" vs. "treat food") and about food plans (why meals are planned to include some of each food group). These nutrition lessons will need to be repeated many times, in more detail, as your children get older and want to understand more about why.

We can begin teaching by explaining about the essential nutrients that every meal needs: protein (including dairy), grains (carbohydrates), fruits and vegetables, and a small amount of fat. The story about Jack at the beginning of this book does just that. It introduces three- to six-year-olds to the names of and need for each of the major nutrients. Parents should reinforce this by teaching and quizzing their youngster at the supermarket and restaurants. Children should also see their parents checking the nutrition information listed on food packaging. When they ask us what we're doing, we have additional opportunities for teaching.

Young children need to know that if they eat just bread, cereal, pasta, or even yogurt instead of a balanced meal, their bodies are missing the other important elements of healthy nutrition. For example, you can demonstrate balanced eating by explaining that a stool with only one or two legs will fall down – it needs at least three supports to stand. *The Edible Pyramid* by Loreen Leedy (Holiday House, 2007) helps teach young children about balanced nutrition. **For specifics on the benefits of each food group,** see Chapter 3 of *Feeding Your Child for Lifelong Health (Birth through Age Six)* by Susan B. Roberts, Ph.D., and Melvin B. Heyman, M.D. (Bantam Books/Random House, 1999); and Chapter 12 of *Helping Your Child Lose Weight the Healthy Way* by Judith Levine, R.D., M.S., and Linda Bine (Citadel Press/Kensington Publishing Co., 2001), or any of the websites listed on page 31.

EATING REGULAR MEALS

Three meals a day served at regular times, usually along with midmorning and midafternoon snacks, can help ensure that your child will be well-nourished. Some youngsters don't need a midmorning snack, and

some need a snack one day but not the next. Parents can experiment with whether to provide one or not. If your child is frequently not hungry enough to eat at meals, check with his other caregivers to make sure that he's not eating too much at snack time or snacking too often. Eating meals and snacks at regular times helps children mentally and physically predict when they'll eat again and ensures that they'll be hungry for the nutritious, balanced meals and healthy snacks you're trying to provide. If dinner is early and bedtime late, some children need a small snack before bedtime. Young children can get grumpy, over-reactive, and fatigued if they go too long between meals, and hunger can contribute to tantrums.

On the other hand, children who eat continuously through the day may get lots of calories but may miss out on a proper balance of nutrients because they're not hungry enough at mealtimes. They may be missing major food groups such as protein, because snacks are not usually as well-balanced as meals are. These "grazers" may also be using food as recreation, out of boredom, or as a way to get their parents' attention. Preschoolers and kindergartners usually need to have two to three hours between meals and snacks to develop sufficient appetite.

Although it's hard to deny your child food when he keeps asking, he can get out of the grazing habit by being guided to do other things, such as crafts projects, helping you with chores, or just playing inside or outside.

PORTION SIZE

For many children, it's best to offer portions that don't seem too big to them. Large portions can seem insurmountable to a child with a small appetite and can make the child give up before starting or feel pressured to eat everything on the plate. That can make her less enthusiastic about eating. Parents can get stressed when the food is wasted. Start out small and offer more if your child is still hungry.

WHAT YOUNG CHILDREN NEED TO EAT

The tables on pages 29-30 show the range of calories young children need, depending on age, gender, and activity level, and show the serving size of the various essential nutrients for children with calorie needs from 1000 to 1600, which is the typical range for two- to six-year-olds. However, a child's appetite varies from day to day, depending on activity level, wellness, sleep etc. Use this information as a guide, but not as a daily absolute.

Examples of child-friendly menus are shown on page 32. Feeding your child as recommended in these tables ensures that you are offering both the kinds and quantities of foods that provide needed nutrients for your growing child. Yet because many children don't like to sit long, want to go and play, or may not be hungry enough, getting young children to eat enough quality food can be a struggle and a source of frustration to parents. This will be addressed throughout this guide.

Remember, the amounts recommended and patterns are based on your child's specific nutrient needs. *Children's intake will vary, based on body build, metabolism, activity level, fatigue, distractions, and other factors.* Eating the same foods you offer your child encourages healthy eating habits – don't forget that you are the role model.

You can find the complete 70-page document *Dietary Guidelines for Americans, 2005* at http://www.health.gov/DietaryGuidelines/ and you can get the next update, 2010 Dietary Guidelines for Americans, in Fall, 2010. (Specific guidelines for children, Spring, 2011).

Calorie Needs Based on Age, Gender, and Activity Level[1]

Activity Level Per Day		Boys			Girls		
		Sedentary less than 30 minutes	Moderately Active 30–60 minutes	Active more than 60 minutes	Sedentary less than 30 minutes	Moderately Active 30–60 minutes	Active more than 60 minutes
Age	2	1000	1000	1000	1000	1000	1000
	3	1000	1400	1400	1000	1200	1400
	4	1200	1400	1600	1200	1400	1400
	5	1200	1400	1600	1200	1400	1600
	6	1400	1600	1800	1200	1400	1600

Nutrition for Preschoolers and Kindergartners[2]

Food Group	Equivalent servings	Serving Size to meet Daily Calorie Requirements			
		1000	1200	1400	1600
Meat and Beans Group					
Includes meat, chicken, turkey, fish, eggs, nut butter, and dry beans. Offer a variety of lean meats and poultry, fish, beans and peas, nuts, and seeds. (Minimize use of processed meats such as luncheon meats, hot dogs, and sausages because of the added sodium.)	**1 ounce equivalents:** 1 ounce of cooked lean meat, chicken, turkey, or fish 1 cooked egg 1 Tablespoon nut butter (peanut or cashew butter) ½ ounce nuts or seeds ¼ cup cooked dry beans (pinto, kidney, white, or black beans) ¼ cup tofu	2 ounces	3 ounces	4 ounces	5 ounces
Milk Group					
Includes all fluid milk products and foods made from milk that retain their calcium content, such as milk, yogurt, and cheese. Foods made from milk that have less than 15% calcium and more fat, such as cream cheese, cream, and butter, are not part of this group. Most milk group choices should be fat-free or low-fat.	**½ cup equivalents:** ½ cup milk ½ cup yogurt ¾ ounce natural cheese (e.g., Swiss) 3 Tablespoons shredded cheese ¼ cup cottage cheese (calcium-fortified) 1 ounce of low-fat processed cheese (e.g., American)	2 cups	2 cups	2 cups	3 cups
Vegetable Group					
All fresh, frozen, canned, and dried vegetables and vegetable juices. Fresh vegetables are recommended over frozen, canned and dried vegetables and are preferred over any juice. Select a variety of brightly colored vegetables, emphasizing dark green, orange, and yellow. Choose vegetables from all of these categories during the week to ensure complete nutrition.	**½ cup equivalents:** ½ cup cooked vegetables (e.g., broccoli, zucchini, green beans) ½ cup raw vegetables (e.g., baby carrots, tomato, zucchini) 1 cup raw leafy greens (lettuce) ½ cup vegetable juice ½ cup cooked potato 1 small ear of corn (6")	1 cup	1½ cups	1½ cups	2 cups

Types of Vegetables		per week			
Dark green vegetables	broccoli, spinach	1 cup	1½ cups	1½ cups	2 cups
Orange vegetables	carrots, winter squash	½ cup	1 cup	1 cup	1½ cups
Legumes	peas, beans	½ cup	1 cup	1 cup	2½ cups
Starchy vegetables	potatoes, corn	1½ cups	2½ cups	2½ cups	2½ cups
Other vegetables	tomatoes, green beans, cucumber	3½ cups	4½ cups	4½ cups	5½ cups

Nutrition for Preschoolers and Kindergartners *(continued)*

Food Group	Equivalent servings	Serving Size to meet Daily Calorie Requirements			
		1000	1200	1400	1600
Fruit Group					
Includes all fresh, frozen, canned, and dried fruits and juices. Fresh fruit is recommended over frozen, canned, or dried fruit and is considered better than any juices.	**½ cup equivalents:** ½ piece of fruit (e.g., apple, orange, mango, peach) ½ banana (8") ½ cup chopped or canned (e.g., strawberries, 4 cut-up medium) ½ bunch grapes (15) ¼ cup dried fruit	1 cup	1 cup	1½ cups	1½ cups
Grains Group					
Includes all foods made from wheat, rice, oats, cornmeal, barley, such as bread, pasta, oatmeal, breakfast cereals, and tortillas. At least half of all grains consumed should be whole grains. (Whole grains include the entire grain kernel.) Refined grains (white flour, white rice) remove some of the nutrient value of grains, especially the fiber. Look for "whole" before the name of the grain, such as "whole wheat."	**½ ounce equivalents:** ½ regular sliced bread ½ cup dry cereal ¼ cup cooked cereal ¼ cup cooked rice ¼ cup cooked pasta 3 square or round crackers ¼ pita bread (6") ½ small tortilla (6") ½ small muffin or 1 rice cake (4") ½ small bagel ½ small biscuit or ½ plain roll 1 small pancake (3") ½ waffle (4½" square) ¼ hamburger or hot dog bun	3 ounces	4 ounces	5 ounces	5 ounces
Oils					
Some oils (fats) are necessary for health. Most dietary fats should come from poly- and mono-unsaturated fats such as plant oils like canola, corn, olive, soybean, and sunflower oils, and from nuts, and some fish, such as salmon. Look for foods low in saturated fat and cholesterol, and with no trans fats.	**1 teaspoon equivalents:** 1 teaspoon oils (plant) ⅛ avocado 1½ teaspoons mayonnaise 1 teaspoon soft margarine 1½ teaspoons salad dressing	3 tsps.	4 tsps.	4 tsps.	5 tsps.
Discretionary Calorie Allowance					
These are the balance of calories remaining in a person's energy allowance after meeting recommended nutrient intake. They can be used to select foods that are not as nutrient dense: foods with additional fats and sugars such as ice cream, cookies, jelly, or other desserts.		165 calories	171 calories	171 calories	132 calories

[1]Although young children are naturally more active than older children and adults because of the running, jumping, and climbing that they do, some children are more sedentary, others more active. For all children, a minimum of an hour a day of physical activity is recommended, beyond their typical activities, for their healthy development (see the Parents' Guidance Section for a fuller explanation of these issues.) This food table is designed to clarify what parents can expect young children to eat, based on their child's age, gender, and activity level. If your child is becoming overweight, then increased activity has to be encouraged along with a closer look at the quality and quantity of your child's food consumption. (www.mypyramid.gov)

[2]Adapted by JoAnn Hattner MPH, RD and Annye Rothenberg PhD, from *Dietary Guidelines for Americans 2005,* U.S. Dept. of Health and Human Services and U.S. Dept. of Agriculture; and from www.mypyramid.gov and www.healthierus.gov/dietaryguidelines. (The next version of the *Dietary Guidelines* is expected in Fall of 2010, and guidelines specifically concerning children in early 2011.)

Further details can be obtained from the following respected websites of government agencies and well-known organizations:

http://www.healthierus.gov/nutrition.html or **www.mypyramid.gov** —*The U.S. Department of Health and Human Services (USDHHS) and the U.S. Department of Agriculture (USDA)*

www.cdc.gov—*U.S. Centers for Disease Control and Prevention*

www.aap.org/obesity   *(American Academy of Pediatrics)*

www.eatright.org—*(American Dietetic Association)*

www.amhrt.org—*(American Heart Association)*

www.hc-sc.gc.ca—*(Health Canada – Ministry of Health)*

SNACKS

Many children want snacks frequently. *It's very hard to say no, but snacks should be limited – both in terms of when and what is served.* Young children don't usually understand nutrition or have the self-control to choose healthy snacks or limit their servings. *Most young children are inclined to demand any food that appeals to them, right now, instead of at a planned snack or meal.* They keep demanding because it's hard for them to understand why we say no, and of course because sometimes we have given in. This is why it's so important to regularly explain about balanced nutrition and develop family rules about the kinds of snack foods you offer. (Remember the one- or two-legged stool mentioned earlier.)

Snacks should be served in smaller portions than meals

and should consist primarily of healthy (nutrient-dense) foods – preferably at least two food groups, so your child's hunger is satisfied until the next meal. Healthful snack foods include fresh or dried fruits and vegetables; bread, crackers, pretzels, rice cakes; and/or protein foods such as peanut butter or hummus, and nonfat or low-fat cheese, yogurt, and milk. Try fruit and string cheese or yogurt. Stocking the house with healthy foods encourages good nutrition, and many parents find it wisest not to keep the tempting, unhealthy treats around at all. It's hard to keep your child away from less healthy foods – like high-sugar, high-salt, high-fat foods – if you keep them in the house. And not having to say no means fewer tantrums.

If you give in to the demand for snacks, it can just make the problem worse. For example, consider this scenario:

Three-year-old Adam had already had his snack. A little later, he asked for another. Dad resisted, but gave in to "just two crackers." Dad left the box out on the counter, and several times, Adam helped himself to more. Then he was thirsty and asked Dad for juice. After that, Dad said that was all he could have, because it was almost dinnertime.

When dinner was served 45 minutes later, Adam ate very little. Then at bedtime, Adam insisted he was starving, and Dad gave him the rest of his dinner. After that, he couldn't fall asleep, because he was re-energized from eating.

The next day, Adam asked for extra snacks, pushing this limit all day. He seemed to have concluded, probably not for the first time, that his daddy can be manipulated into not enforcing the rules.

CURBING CUPBOARD RAIDING

Many children will help themselves to food as soon as they are old enough to open the refrigerator and cabinets. *But most young children don't make good decisions about what to eat.* You'll need to explain to your child why he can't just help himself without asking. Supervise him closely so he knows you mean what you say. If the requested food fits into the next snack or meal, you can say yes and tell him why, *and* when he'll be able to have it, so he understands your rules. Otherwise, a child can get used to having too much say in deciding what and when to eat, and when you have to tell him no, he may

Sample Menus at the 1200- and 1400-calorie Levels

1200 calories a day

Includes: 4 oz. grains, 1½ cups vegetables, 1 cup fruit, 3 oz. meat/beans, 2 cups milk, and 4 tsp. oil

	Actual Amount	Food Group Equivalent
Breakfast	½ cup cooked oatmeal	1 oz. grain
	¼ cup dried fruit (e.g., raisins)	½ cup fruit
	½ cup milk	½ cup milk
Midmorning	3 crackers (whole grain)	½ oz. grain
	½ ounce nuts	1 oz. meat/beans
	½ cup milk	½ cup milk
Lunch	English muffin pizza	
	½ English muffin	1 oz. grain
	1 T pizza sauce*	
	3 T shredded cheese	½ cup milk
	1 cup raw vegetables (e.g., celery, carrots, green, red and yellow peppers)	1 cup vegetables
	½ medium fresh fruit (e.g., apple)	½ cup fruit
	water	
Midafternoon	2 medium pretzels	½ oz. grain
	½ cup milk	½ cup milk
Dinner	2 oz. baked, broiled or grilled salmon (or other fish, meat, or poultry)	2 oz. meat/beans
	½ cup cooked rice	1 oz. grain
	½ cup squash (e.g., zucchini)	½ cup vegetables
	½ cup ice cream*	
	water	

1400 calories a day

Includes: 5 oz. grains, 1½ cups vegetables, 1½ cups fruit, 4 oz. meat/beans, 2 cups milk, and 4 tsp. oil

	Actual Amount	Food Group Equivalent
Breakfast	1 cup unsweetened cereal	1 oz. grain
	with ½ cup milk	½ cup milk
	½ cup strawberries	½ cup fruit
	1 scrambled egg	1 oz. meat/beans
Midmorning	2 graham crackers	1 oz. grain
	1 T nut butter	1 oz. meat/beans
	water	
Lunch	Grilled cheese sandwich	
	2 slices bread (whole grain)	2 oz. grain
	1 ½ oz. cheese	1 cup milk
	½ cup baby carrots	½ cup vegetables
	½ banana	½ cup fruit
	water	
Midafternoon	1 rice cake	½ oz. grain
	½ cup yogurt	½ cup milk
	½ orange	½ cup fruit
	water	
Dinner	2 oz. baked, broiled or grilled chicken (or fish, meat)	2 oz. meat/beans
	1 corn-on-the-cob	½ cup vegetables
	½ cup broccoli	½ cup vegetables
	¼ cup cooked pasta	½ oz. grain
	3 small cookies*	

* Discretionary (or extra) calories: Most items on the 1200-calorie and 1400-calorie menus are low-fat and contain no added sugar. Foods higher in fats and sugars are marked with an asterisk (*) and should be included in "discretionary calories." Those make up about 170 additional calories above the basic diet for the day. Those calories may come from additional quantities of foods in the regular diet, or from modest quantities of "splurge" foods with additional fats and sugars, such as desserts and snacks. Use the nutrition label to determine the calories in those foods, gauging the quantities carefully.

Oils represent amounts added during manufacturing, cooking, or at the table.

These sample menus were prepared by JoAnn Hattner, MPH, RD, and Annye Rothenberg, PhD, as examples of nutritionally balanced eating. Other examples of healthy *and* unhealthy menus, actual food logs, and information on how to improve your child's nutritional balance can be found in these books: *Feeding Your Child for Lifelong Health (birth to six years)* by Susan B. Roberts, PhD, and Melvin B. Heyman, MD (Bantam Books/Random House, 1999), and *Helping Your Child Lose Weight the Healthy Way* by Judith Levine, RD, MS and Linda Bine (Citadel Press/Kensington Publishing, Co. 2001).

feel entitled to sneak food. If a child is very focused on taking his own food, see if you can figure out why he's doing it when he's not really hungry. You'll need to remind him that you're in charge, and why. Also make sure that his meals are balanced and served at regular times. Help him find ways to keep occupied. Keeping busy and active, and spending time with you, can fill your child's emotional needs better than food can.

When your child has other caregivers at your home, they need to know your rules around food and your reasons. The children need to hear you explain this to the caregivers, including suggestions for activities to redirect the children toward when they're nagging for treats. Even at your child's nursery school, kindergarten, or child care center, you may need to explain your food rules and reasons to the teachers.

LIQUID CONSUMPTION

Milk and water are the important liquids for children to drink. About 16 to 24 ounces daily of dairy products are recommended (depending on the age, gender, and activity level – see the tables on pages 29-30), along with unlimited water. Juices are no longer considered to be good nutrition, but fruit is.

Make sure your child is not filling up on milk, which by itself doesn't provide balanced nutrition for this age. Preschoolers and kindergartners no longer need milk before breakfast or just before bed. This can decrease a child's appetite – especially for breakfast. Keep track of your child's daily milk consumption if she has a

limited appetite for food. For picky eaters, it's especially important to limit intake to the recommended amount. Provide small amounts of milk and don't provide seconds till the child has eaten enough food. Sodas (soft drinks) and sports drinks (like Gatorade) are not recommended by pediatric dietitians as they provide empty calories, meaning they contain no essential nutrients. Sports drinks were developed for adults doing sustained, vigorous, lengthy exercise.

Children can be very demanding about wanting what adults drink, especially soda and sports drinks. Parents need to model healthy behavior for their children, and recognize that heavy consumption of those drinks is not healthy at any age. Some children may also show interest in adult drinks such as coffee, or even wine or beer. Parents should emphasize, "This is only for grown-ups," and explain why.

It's important for everyone to drink water many times a day. Having water easily available for your child and drinking it yourself encourages this habit. An accessible sink with a stool or an easy-to-use dispenser with readily available cups both work well. Frequent water consumption, if it's not common in your home, is easiest to teach during the summer when everyone is much more likely to be thirsty.

INTRODUCING NEW FOODS

One way to teach about nutrition is to expand your child's food experiences. Offer your children *new* foods regularly even if they aren't adventurous eaters, and let them see you eating them. *Variety is important for both complete nutrition and taste appeal.* Parents may need to offer the same new food many times before their children will try it. You can involve your child more in food shopping *and* preparation so he can see food more as a "friend." He will be more likely to try it *and* he'll see you eating what he made. For your reluctant or cautious child's benefit, try commenting *out loud* on your own reactions to the new foods: "I don't know if I'm going to like this. It's really good for my body, so I think I'll just give it a little lick. Not bad. I'll give it a little bite. Hmm, I think it's pretty good, especially if I eat it with something on it. I'll put ketchup on it."

It would create too much pressure to keep talking about trying the new food all through the meal (or worse, all day). On the other hand, you want to actively

encourage your child to try new foods. Try to make it fun to talk about new foods, to help young children relax and cooperate. Reasoning and logical explanations usually are not enough encouragement for preschoolers, and sometimes not even for kindergartners. You can get more interest by **talking for the food** and giving it a bit of a personality: broccoli that wants to be eaten now ("I want to be picked first!"), bread that says "don't put any more butter on me, please!" or wants to be eaten last, etc. It's helpful for kids to experience new foods, watch you eat, and enjoy your humorous approach.

Kids love cooking, so have your child help you cook, as messy and slow as that is for you. That will provide some extra fun time with him, and he'll be more likely to eat food he helped create.

MAKING FOOD VISUALLY APPEALING

Children enjoy colorful foods. Emphasizing the natural rainbow of colors in foods encourages children to appreciate a variety of foods for maximum nutritional and visual appeal – the more colors the better. Decorating foods is also fun (such as a happy face made of blueberries on a pancake). It's good to have some familiar foods (in small quantities) the child already likes on her plate when you offer a new food. Flavorings like cheese, ketchup, salad dressings, or light salting or seasoning help some children to try more new foods: Show them how to dip vegetables into ranch or other salad dressing, fruit into yogurt, and meat, fish, and poultry into ketchup.

VITAMIN SUPPLEMENTS

Parents can feel confused about whether their children need vitamin supplements. A balanced diet based on the USDHHS and USDA Dietary Guidelines (see the information on pages 29-30) contains sufficient vitamins and minerals for your young child. Most children in the U.S. get enough vitamins and minerals because so many basic foods are fortified with them. However, pediatricians may advise parents to give multivitamins to children who have very limited diets. If you are uncertain, keep a food log for three consecutive days and show it to your pediatrician to get advice.

• SECTION TWO •
ESSENTIALS FOR SUCCESSFUL EATING BEHAVIOR

Eating as a family and practicing good nutrition and table manners make it easier for young children to learn about and enjoy healthy foods. Setting eating rules and involving your child in food preparation can help him develop healthier eating habits.

Some children like a wide variety of foods, have good appetites, and stay seated at the table long enough to eat a good meal or snack. Many don't. As in other aspects of their life, children are playful, happy little scientists experimenting with their world. Food to them can be an interesting and potentially fun kind of crafts project but can also test parents' limits and patience.

PAGING MISS MANNERS

Young children don't know that there are rules about eating until you teach them. If young children had a choice, many would prefer to leave the table and come back and get more when they wanted to, though not necessarily because they were hungry. They'd walk around the house eating and drinking as they go. Many would disrupt the meal by playing with their food or climbing on our laps to eat from our plates. Children request other food, then change their minds and pick yet a different food. Because all this is natural for young children, there are a lot of table rules to teach.

Young children don't learn eating behavior or nutrition on their own. Parents need to set eating rules at home that are similar to those expected in the community, such as at school, in restaurants, and in other homes. Because young children's preferred eating behavior usually is not acceptable, they require lots of mealtime training. It's easier to teach expectations to a child who is hungry at mealtimes and is not given a lot of choice about what to eat. Parents need to teach their children to stay at the table, eat with utensils, say please and thank you, and not push food off their plates, spill things, throw or drop food, or do "chemistry experiments" with their food. We need to help our children learn to enjoy the meal and conversation enough that mealtimes are not filled with their out-of-bounds behavior and/or our threats and consequences.

Most parents have to decide on a reasonable length of time for children to stay at the table, especially for children who always finish eating before the rest of the family. Younger preschoolers can usually stay seated for 10 minutes and older preschoolers and kindergartners for 20 minutes. However, you should look for signs that your child has had enough to eat. That's when children become bored and when most behavior problems begin. Clear rules, enforced consistently, and **immediate consequences** help children know what's expected at meals. Once they have learned the rules, most mealtimes can go quite well.

These are reasonable goals. The rest of Section Two explains how to work toward them. When you do, the family will find mealtimes more satisfying and less stressful, curbing both your emotional outbursts and your child's.

MAKING MEALTIME KID-FRIENDLY

Your child needs to be hungry enough, be seated comfortably, have an adult eat with her, and be engaged in the conversation. She also needs to like at least some of the food being served, and not be served portions that look too big (which makes her feel she can't be "successful" at eating what you want her to eat). Don't watch TV, take or make calls, read, or work on your computer while you're eating with your children. That can easily make your children feel ignored and unimportant.

SEATING COMFORTABLY

After your child outgrows his highchair, usually around two to two and a half, he needs a seat that will put him at the right height for the table and make him comfortable enough to stay seated and eat. Some families use booster seats. For children ages two through seven,

chairs with adjustable seats and foot platforms for use at a table are available at many stores that sell children's items. The seat should be padded and there should be back and foot support so it is easier for him to stay seated. You can use an existing chair and nail a board across the front legs to make a platform for your child's feet. If the chair is uncomfortable and his feet are dangling, you can expect much more difficulty with your youngster's table behavior.

ACCOMMODATING FIDGETERS

Lots of eating behavior problems can be prevented. Make sure children have enough running-around time so they can sit longer at meals. Parents should try to notice when their children are no longer hungry and/or are tired or fidgety. Trying to make the meal a little shorter or having less food on the plate helps prevent behavior problems. Since many children would like shorter meals with less food, even though the amount they're eating isn't sufficient for them, it's best if you make modifications to your expectations as early in the meal as possible. That way you can decrease spilling, negotiations, and refusals. You can also make the meal more interesting for your child with conversation on kid-friendly topics or with the "talking food" game described earlier ("The carrot says, 'I don't want to lie on your plate. I want to be in your tummy' "). Preschoolers really enjoy the "talking game," and kindergartners usually smile.

RULES

Mealtime rules are necessary. Basic rules for young children might be: You have to eat at the table. No walking around with food. You have to stay until you're excused. Use your fork and spoon. No playing with your

food. No blowing bubbles with your drinks. No pushing the plate away. No screaming. These are just examples. Parents need to decide what makes sense and develops the good habits they want their children to have at home and in the community. *Both parents have to agree on the rules if they are to be effective.* A child needs to be hungry enough and have had enough exercise so she is less fidgety at the table. Parents need to sit and eat with their children and converse with them during the meal, and there need to be consequences for misbehavior.

CONVERSING WITH YOUR YOUNG CHILD

We want to help our children socialize at mealtime. Talking about the day with your family at mealtimes begins at the preschool age when children are old enough to have a conversation. We want to talk about subjects that youngsters easily understand and enjoy. Meals should not be just parents talking to each other. Ask your child about his trip to the library or have him tell Dad about his playdate. Try *not* to ask question after question just to get your curiosity satisfied and your worries diminished. *A one-sided series of queries is not conversation*: Did you listen to your teacher? Did you eat your lunch? Did you stay in circle? Did you do the crafts project? Who did you play with? Model taking turns talking and not interrupting. This is how we set a lifetime pattern of connecting

at meals as a family. We want mealtime socializing to be enjoyable.

CONSEQUENCES

When preschoolers are playing with their food and getting up and down instead of eating, ask yourself why your eating behavior training isn't working. You may be issuing many reminders and threats but putting off the decisive action of sending her away from the table, in the hope that she'll eat more if she stays. *However, too many warnings and threats without action convince your child that she doesn't need to listen to you.* Some parents remove the child's plate or take her to time-out. Others move the child away from the family to a separate little table. You may have to go further, especially if your child misbehaves at the little table or just keeps misbehaving at the family table. The most effective method for showing your child you mean what you say is, after a warning, to scrape the food from her plate down the garbage disposal so she knows there's no second chance. This is a useful method when you know she is still hungry but she's not focused enough on eating. Putting her food down the disposal is dramatic because it's so final – quite different from leaving the food on the table or counter, or putting it in the refrigerator for later. Children are usually so bothered by this that parents rarely have to do it more than one or two times. Expect her to be so shocked and outraged that you may have to send her to time-out for a while.

If your child isn't especially hungry, putting her food down the disposal probably wouldn't bother her and therefore is not the method to use. Instead, you'll probably have to think back on – and check with her other caregivers about – when and how much she has eaten, especially snacks. Consider the other important reasons as well – too tired; physically uncomfortable at the table; hasn't had enough exercise; or a stressful atmosphere. See what you and the other caregivers need to do differently so your child can eat better at mealtimes.

SETTING GUIDELINES, STAYING FIRM

Parents often feel conflicted about what foods to offer their young children and how much to expect them to eat. Above all, parents want their children to get enough quality nutrition and calories at meals and snacks so they grow well. Children need enough energy to play and learn. Parents want their children to eat enough that they feel comfortably full and don't keep asking for food. On the other hand, parents don't want their children to become overweight and, probably, less active and less healthy. Young children realize how strongly their parents feel about food. They are also old enough to begin learning that some foods are better for them than others – that chicken is healthier than cookies and fruit is healthier than candy.

Children who have low interest in eating or sitting because they have small appetites or because they're extremely active will likely try to get their parents to compromise their mealtime expectations. Badgered, tired parents might give their child less nutritious foods than they know they should, just to get something into his stomach. They may give in to his demand to sit on their lap and eat from their plates or to leave the table and come back over and over. They may even leave his plate of food out in an effort to get him to eat enough.

Then there are the frustrated parents of overeaters, who may find themselves acquiescing when their children repeatedly ask for more food or less healthy food. Of course, every parent compromises mealtime rules when rushed or when a child is sick, but giving in frequently results in more troublesome mealtime behavior that can surface as soon as the next meal.

It's very hard for parents to insist that their child eat what's prepared or else go hungry. (We all know that few children or adults like every food that's served.) It's even hard to say no to the occasionally served dessert for your child because he didn't eat enough healthy food. When a child is upset or demanding, it's difficult for parents to focus on the long-term learning that needs to be established. **It helps to explain to your youngster that he needs healthy food to give him energy, keep him from getting sick and help his body grow.** Use humor to let him know the chicken, broccoli, and strawberries want to be in his tummy. And you can use compassion and redirection when he sees everyone else having ice cream: "It's hard to watch Daddy and your sister eating ice cream. You really wanted some, too, and it doesn't seem fair. But we can only have a treat if we've had enough good and healthy food. We'll try again tomorrow. Let's go read your favorite book instead." In the next section, you'll find many useful ways to help picky eaters and, in Section Four, overeaters.

• SECTION THREE •
PICKY EATING

"I ALREADY KNOW I DON'T LIKE IT!"

Decreased appetites and increased independence make young children more inclined to be picky eaters. Although some children have a highly sensitive sense of smell, taste, and/or texture, this isn't the case with most picky eaters. Children often become picky about food because their parents unintentionally over-accommodate their preferences. When parents start telling their kids they're picky eaters, children may use this as an excuse and a label. Most parents aren't prepared for the normal decrease in appetite between one and three years of age, and they become intent on trying to get any calories at all into their children. Sometimes parents give in to avoid their children's emotional upsets at meals. These children become selective and demanding in their food choices and often end up consuming too much milk, juice, or sweet and/or salt-fat foods. That makes healthier foods (with less salt-fat or sugar) taste less appealing to them. Children who eat too frequently may also become picky because they are never hungry enough to eat what's offered. It's so hard to say no when your child asks for food, but parents need to remember that if she eats now, she most likely won't be hungry for dinner in half an hour.

James had eaten everything when he was a baby and liked a variety of foods as a young toddler. But by age two, he had become increasingly picky. Now, at four, James would eat a waffle with lots of syrup for breakfast; he wanted gummy fruit treats and crackers for snacks; and for lunch and dinner, he insisted on grilled cheese or macaroni and cheese. Sometimes he would eat a jelly sandwich. His only vegetables or fruits were an occasional carrot or banana. James drank three or four eight-ounce sippy cups of milk a day. His parents, Cynthia and Wes, offered him many foods, but he refused them. They tried bribing him with candy or potato chips to try chicken or zucchini. But that didn't work, and James always demanded desserts of cookies or ice cream.

Eventually, James' food choices had narrowed to only a few items that didn't provide enough nutritional balance. Cynthia and Wes were worried and frustrated, and James' pediatrician was getting concerned about his nutrition. It was hard to take James to a friend's home or a restaurant. They knew they had to do something, because it looked like James was getting bored of these foods too, and they feared that he might soon stop eating entirely.

The pediatrician advised Cynthia and Wes to record everything that James ate and drank and also to look at their own eating habits. When they did, they realized James was getting most of his calories from milk, starting with the cup he had when he first woke up. An honest look at themselves revealed that Cynthia and Wes didn't eat balanced meals, didn't enjoy food preparation, and didn't sit very long at meals. In fact, James usually ate by himself while his parents were listening to their phone messages and checking their e-mail.

James' parents followed their pediatrician's recommendation to cut back to 16 ounces of milk a day, including cheese and yogurt – a common guideline for this age. (As much as 24 ounces may be appropriate for some children.) They offered water instead at meals. They brought the cup out only when it was time to drink rather than making it available at all times. Cynthia and Wes began spending more time on food preparation and involved James in the process so he would get used to other kinds of food. As they cut his milk consumption, he had more appetite at meals. They gave him small amounts of his favorite foods and introduced small portions of new foods flavored with appealing tastes such as salad dressing and ketchup. They worked on their own nutrition, prepared more balanced meals, and began to sit and eat with James at meals. After several months, they began to talk to him about healthy and treat foods. They offered him fewer sweet and salty snacks. This made the more nutritious foods taste better. His increased appetite made James more adventurous with new food and more willing to try new foods. With time and firm patience, Cynthia and Wes helped James expand his food variety and make eating more social and enjoyable – for them too. As a result, his insistence on treats and their worry about his nutrition (and even theirs) decreased.

If your child is very demanding as you're making dinner, the best food to offer is raw vegetables, with a dip such as ranch dressing if it encourages your child to eat them. She is more likely to try vegetables when she's very hungry than at dinner where other foods are on her plate. Vegetables are less filling than many other kinds of foods and are so healthy and low in calories that it won't matter even if she eats a little less of her meal.

AVOIDING THE ALLURE OF FOODS WITH TOO MUCH SUGAR, SALT, AND FAT

Children often prefer sweet and/or salt-fat foods because they taste so good. Eating those foods tends to produce cravings for more, and too much of them makes healthier foods seem less tasty and appealing. The whole family should work to avoid making sweets a habit (candy, cookies, ice cream, doughnuts, cake). And if your child is eating a lot of crackers, chips, French fries, chicken nuggets, and other high-salt and high-fat foods, cut these foods back so that more nutritious foods don't lose their appeal. Fruits, which are usually naturally sweet, can be offered as part of the meal (or as a dessert). Some families are giving fruit and yogurt for dessert and calling them "treats," to help children focus less on nutritionally poor foods. You can prepare fruit kebabs, fruit salad, or kiwi slices with raisin eyes. A major problem with fast-food restaurants and processed foods from the supermarket is that it's hard to resist the many items in the overly salt-fat or sweet category.

At first, it can seem impossible to decrease the salt, fat, and sugar foods in your child's diet if that's all she will eat. But go slowly and keep trying. Cravings can be modified dramatically. Set limits on those foods so your child can't fill up on them. Then eliminate them from most meals and allow them just in one afternoon snack or after dinner each day – so the other foods at the meal don't seem less enticing by comparison. When high-sugar, high-salt, and high-fat foods are decreased with time, other more nutritious foods will taste good and be satisfying enough.

MAY I PLEASE HAVE SECONDS?

If your child wants seconds of his preferred food, you can encourage him to eat some of the other foods first (at least three bites). This is especially important if your child's preferred foods are high-carbohydrate foods like bread or pasta, which children often love and fill up on. (Note: Specially manufactured low-carb foods don't provide the proper balance for children's nutritional needs.)

MAKING SEPARATE MEALS

When parents continually make separate meals for their children, or get up during the meal to make something

their child prefers to what's on her plate, they are inadvertently enabling their child's food choices to become more individualized, demanding, and limited. *If a child needs special food for a good reason and can't make it herself, you could have her help you prepare the main meal so that she learns that the privilege of having special meals comes with extra work.* Otherwise, children can become very demanding and self-centered about their food – assuming that you can "short-order cook" what they want, whenever they want it. It's generally better, when possible, for parents not to routinely prepare other foods or give other food choices, except of course in the case of food allergies and other dietary restrictions.

If your child is at the table insisting on a separate food or meal, and some explanation and redirection doesn't work, you can send her to her room for creating a scene during a family meal. Later, when her time-out is over, she may be more willing to try the food since she no longer has an audience for her acting-up at the table, and she may be hungrier by then.

BEWARE THE ENERGY BAR

Sometimes parents offer their children food that was developed to be eaten only occasionally by rushed adults. Energy bars or any other "meal in a bar" -type products are not considered a young child's food because they are high in sugar (or use a sugar substitute) – even if they're high in vitamins – and can skew a child's taste preferences away from a wider variety of nutritious foods. Be careful of energy bars. They encourage the idea that food needs can be met that way. Preparing snack bags of healthier food items would be preferable when parents are on the run (string cheese, berries, zucchini spears). Prepare them ahead of time so you can grab a few of these healthier snack packs on your way out of the house.

INVOLVE CHILDREN IN GROWING AND PREPARING FOOD

Children love planting gardens and watching the food grow. Looking forward to picking and finally eating it has a very positive effect on children's attitudes toward food. And children enjoy food more if they help to prepare and serve it, and even help to decorate the table. Children as young as two and a half can wash fruits and vegetables, help tear lettuce, cut soft fruits for a salad, or put spices (under supervision!) on fish, poultry, and meat. *Cooking is fun for children and is a good parent-child activity.* A young child's "help" slows things down, but if you wait until your child is old enough to be an efficient helper, he won't be in the habit of helping out and is likely to resist. You may also lose an opportunity to teach him about cooking and nutrition at an early age. Try to find a small cooking job that he can help you with. A useful book on parents and preschoolers cooking together is *Pretend Soup and Other Real Recipes* by Mollie Katzen and Ann Henderson (Ten Speed Press, 2004).

If your child has prepared the food, he can take center stage talking about it and how he made it. Children who prepare food regard it more as a friend than an enemy. They encounter taste experiences that make them more comfortable with food, partly because it's associated with being with caring adults.

In some families, the concern is not the child who eats too few things but the child who overeats.

• SECTION FOUR •
CURBING OVEREATERS' APPETITES

GAINING TOO MUCH WEIGHT

For children over two years, your pediatrician will use the Body Mass Index (BMI) as a guide to know if your child's weight is healthy for her height. The BMI is based on height, weight, and gender. If you and your pediatrician agree that your child is gaining weight too quickly, based on growth charts showing the BMI, your pediatrician will advise you on what to do. Percentiles from 5th to 85th are considered healthy. Eighty-fifth to 95th is overweight and greater than 95th is obese. The 5th percentile or less is also considered unhealthy. Some pediatricians will want to discuss eating issues with you if your child is 70th percentile or higher. To get the BMI, you need to know your child's height and weight. Various websites offer *automatic BMI calculators,* but make sure to use one *for children*. Here are three choices:

U.S. Centers for Disease Control and Prevention
BMI Calculator for Child and Teens
http://apps.nccd.cdc.gov/dnpabmi/calculator.aspx

www.keepkidshealthy.com
BMI Calculator
http://www.keepkidshealthy.com/welcome/bmicalculator.html

www.about.com: Pediatrics
BMI Calculator: Are your kids over or underweight?
http://pediatrics.about.com/cs/usefultools/l/bl_bmi_calc.htm

To ensure a healthy BMI, parents need to encourage and participate with their children in more active time – including active indoor and outdoor daily family play time. The easiest is to turn on music and have family dance time. This helps your child find interests besides food as well as helping her make exercise a habit. Young children, in general, need an hour or more of very active play every day to keep them healthy and their appetite in balance. This is essential if your child is sedentary, with a naturally low activity level. The hour is a total for the day – not necessarily all at once – and for sedentary kids, it's challenging. **We need to make physical activity with our youngsters a daily habit, just like cleaning up our toys, putting on clean clothes, and flushing the toilet.** With time, physical activity becomes fun, because it makes children and adults feel good. Enough physical exercise can help the balance of food intake and growth, and help your child's emotional balance, self-control, coordination, ability to focus, and quality of sleep as well.

You should also pay attention to the quality and quantity of foods the entire family eats. Overeaters often become too sedentary, encouraging eating as recreation! Eating meals and snacks in front of the television can make the whole family more inclined to overeat. **A child eating in front of the TV is not being emotionally fulfilled by the social activity of eating with others and may not notice how much she has eaten.** Eat with your children, but make sure that's not the only time they get your best-quality attention. It may be helpful to encourage overeaters to eat vegetables while waiting for dinner and drink their water or milk as they eat to help them feel full at that meal.

Caregivers such as day-care providers, babysitters, and nannies should be given guidelines and suggestions for what, when, and how much your child can eat. Caregivers also need to know ways to meet your child's other needs so he doesn't focus on food as the highlight of his day.

Young children don't have the self-discipline to make good choices about what they eat. Reminders and nagging

Molly loved to eat. She loved big meals and lots of snacks. Her parents, Claire and Alan, often served her favorites – crackers, sandwiches, pasta, cookies, and ice cream. Molly always wanted more. At age five and a half, Molly was noticeably overweight. (Alan also liked eating a lot and was about 35 pounds overweight.) Molly's teacher said she was the last to leave the snack table and often asked the other kids for their food after she had finished hers.

Her parents had tried to limit her snacking, telling her, "Too much food isn't good for you. It's making your tummy get too big." Molly didn't like being told she had a big tummy. She yelled at Daddy that he had a big tummy too. She frequently looked in the mirror and pressed her tummy in. Molly began sneaking into the kitchen and standing on a chair to get snacks. When her parents asked, "What are you doing? Did you just eat something?" Molly would deny it. Claire and Alan were at a loss. They didn't want to punish her, lock up the cupboards, or get rid of all snack foods, as they enjoyed these foods themselves. But they knew Molly's overeating was becoming a big problem. Eating had become her favorite activity – her favorite way to fill time – just as it was Dad's. Neither parent had developed an appreciation for exercise. They enjoyed being home a lot too – playing blocks, puzzles, or dolls with Molly and reading to her. They all enjoyed a lot of screen time, and Molly watched television for several hours every day. Socializing for them focused on food. Outings involved a lot of car trips but not walking, biking, or sports.

They started to read about young children's nutritional needs and realized they were feeding Molly too much – particularly too many carbohydrates. They learned that Molly's high carbohydrate consumption caused her to crave more sweets, and the family's sedentary habits as well as Dad's overeating pushed her toward food as an activity.

Claire and Alan decided to take action. They began serving more balanced meals, decreasing the carbohydrates. They found ways to be more active themselves and with their daughter: They played active games with her, had her help with chores, started doing more physical activities together, went on more exercise-oriented outings, and had more playdates. They all discovered how much fun it was to dance at home to exciting music. They began to enthusiastically suggest other ideas – such as crafts projects – when she was asking for food. Little by little, the changes at home made Molly's life more balanced, and better nutrition made her feel more emotionally and physiologically satisfied so that food began to play a smaller, more normal role in her life. Over the next year, her weight also began to come back into normal range. And so did her Dad's.

by their parents intensify the child's emotional stress, often triggering a desire for more food. See if your child's emotional needs can be met in other ways:

Does she have regular mealtimes with you instead of eating alone, whether at the table or in front of the TV?

Does she have enough cuddling and loving words and actions from you? Does she have regular playtime with you?

Do you need to involve her more with you when you're doing laundry and other household activities?

Has she learned to find interesting things to do on her own?

Have you provided enough intellectually stimulating opportunities?

Does she need more playdates?

Are you doing physical activities with her like putting on music you all can dance to, walking and biking, or kicking balls in your yard or at the park?

Are you pressuring or rushing her too much?

Is there a lot of family tension?

An outstanding book for parents about children's healthy eating and exercise is *Helping Your Child Lose Weight the Healthy Way* by Judith Levine, R.D, M.S., and Linda Bine (Citadel Press/Kensington Publishing Co., 2001). Also see American Academy of Pediatrics' *A Parent's Guide to Childhood Obesity*, by Sandra Hassink, M.D., 2006.

• SECTION FIVE •
MONITORING YOUR CHILD'S NUTRITION

In general, what a child eats in a single meal is not as important as what he eats in a day. And what he eats in a day is not as important as what he eats in a few days. Activity level, metabolism, body build, and fatigue affect how much your child eats. Tired or sick children don't eat well. However, you don't want to lose sight of good nutrition. ***It can be useful for parents to prepare a food log for three to five consecutive days of what, when, and how much their children eat and drink***. Include weekdays and weekend days. Be precise. Guesses and estimates are often very far off. Do this twice a year, to observe the quality and quantity of your child's eating. If you feel your child's nutrition is not sufficiently balanced, you can learn how to modify it through discussion with your child's pediatrician, a pediatric dietitian, or through reading more on children's nutrition. This way, poor eating habits won't become permanent. Look at the next example and try to figure out the problems in this child's diet.

EXAMPLE:
FOOD LOG FROM A FIVE-YEAR-OLD GIRL

DAY ONE:

BREAKFAST	SNACK	LUNCH	SNACK	DINNER
Cheerios, dry without milk (1 bowl)	Pretzels (6 small)	Peanut butter sandwich w/honey on wheat bread	Granola bar	Plain pasta with butter (2 cups)
Juice (6 oz.)	Popsicle	Milk (6 oz.) Banana Gummy bears (8)		2 baby carrots Juice (4 oz.)

DAY TWO:

BREAKFAST	SNACK	LUNCH	SNACK	DINNER
Two waffles w/syrup	Granola bar	Peanut butter w/honey on 2 rice cakes	Banana Popsicle	Cheese pizza (2 slices)
Milk (4 oz.)		Juice (4 oz.) Potato chips (1½ cups) Water		Juice (6 oz.)

This two-day food log shows several important things. The five-year-old's diet was very low in protein, including milk and dairy products, and in fruits and vegetables. There were too many sweets and salt foods, skewing her taste preferences away from milk and other protein foods and from fruits and vegetables. Her parents will need to dramatically decrease and preferably eliminate juice as well as most of the sweets and salty snacks. With less juice, she's likely to increase her consumption of water and milk. With fewer sweets and salt-fat foods, all other foods start to taste better. Her meals need more variety rather than oversized quantities of one item. Breakfast could include cereal, eggs, French toast, or waffles with fruit and milk, etc. Lunch should include vegetables and fruit along with a wider range of sandwiches. Dinner should include meat, poultry or fish with vegetables, fruit, and carbohydrates. For sample meals, see page 32. For information on snacks, see page 31.

FOR FURTHER READING

An excellent book on overall nutrition is *Feeding Your Child for Lifelong Health (Birth through Age Six)* by Susan B. Roberts, Ph.D., and Melvin B. Heyman, M.D. (Bantam Books/Random House, 1999). *Helping Your Child Lose Weight the Healthy Way* by Judith Levine, R.D, M.S., and Linda Bine (Citadel Press/Kensington Publishing Co.,

2001) is also an excellent book, focusing on overeaters, and look at American Academy of Pediatrics' *A Parent's Guide to Childhood Obesity* by Sandra Hassink, M.D., 2006. These books, along with the USDA's Dietary Guidelines for Americans, 2005, and its regular five-year updates, and the information from other reliable and valuable nutrition websites (see page 31), will help you understand what kinds of foods and what quantities constitute a healthy diet for a young child. (Also, see pages 29-30.)

Nutrition recommendations change more than many other areas of child-rearing such as limit-setting, sleep, social skills, or toilet training. It's hard for parents to rely on their own judgment because of the complex biology and chemistry involved in nutrition, and because new information is frequently published. Some of it actually reverses what had been previously accepted as fundamentals. For example, even 100% fruit juice, previously recommended, is now viewed as insufficient nutritionally. This makes it harder to keep up with nutrition and to feel sure about your knowledge. Reading reliable websites and books, or attending lectures, can be very helpful. A consultation with a dietitian may help you get your questions answered and make you feel more confident. As we read the latest findings in nutrition, we have to use our judgment about whether the information makes sense, and then we wait to see if it's accepted by reliable nutrition and pediatric organizations and knowledgeable professionals.

Limit-setting is also important in guiding children's eating and nutrition habits. For comprehensive, practical guidance on setting child-rearing limits, how to get cooperation, and using consequences, see *Mommy and Daddy Are Always Supposed to Say Yes—Aren't They?* and *Why Do I Have To?*, by this author.

These books on limit-setting will teach you many skills, such as helping your upset child by speaking sympathetically – "It's so hard to learn the new mealtime rules; they really make you mad." You'll learn to tell him what to say when he's angry – "I'm mad that I can't have more bread now" – and how to redirect him – "We can't have a treat now, but here's what we can do." And you'll learn how to use a wide range of consequences when needed – some that we know: and many that are new. "It's never OK to throw your plate. Now we have a lot of cleanup to do. That's going to use up so much time, I'm sad that we won't have time to build our blocks together."

• CONCLUSION •

Helping your children eat well is an important goal. Discovering what you can do to improve your children's eating is satisfying and valuable for parents. As you teach your preschoolers about healthy foods and the role of treat or "splurge" foods, about good eating behavior, and how to incorporate exercise into their day, you are laying the foundation for a healthier, higher-quality life for your children. *Starting your children on the road to understanding the importance of the right balance of food and the importance of exercise is an essential key to taking care of themselves throughout their lives.*

• GUIDELINES FOR TEACHING YOUNG CHILDREN ABOUT HEALTHY EATING •

These guidelines highlight the essentials for young children's healthy eating and exercise habits.

ONE: *Children Don't Naturally Know Which Foods Are Healthy To Eat*

Parents need to begin teaching good nutrition to their children during the preschool years. Preschoolers and kindergartners can begin to learn the need for different types of foods. To do this well, parents often need to learn more and practice better nutrition themselves. Keep up with the current thinking about nutrition. Use books by professionals in the field and be sure that food websites you consult are prepared by professionals in pediatric nutrition and pediatrics.

TWO: *Good Appetite Depends On Many Factors*

How much a child eats depends on his hunger, body build, metabolism, activity level, wellness, fatigue, state of mind, and many other factors. Help your child to have a better appetite by making sure he has enough sleep and lots of exercise. Expect that your child's appetite will be different from meal to meal and day to day.

THREE: *Appetites Vary From One Child To Another*

Be aware of differences in gender and activity level, and know the serving sizes recommended at different ages. (See the tables in this guide, pages 29-30.) Be sure your expectations about how much each of your children should eat are realistic.

FOUR: *Make Mealtimes And Snacktimes Predictable*

Teach your child that we eat at certain times. It's unwise to allow young children free access to the refrigerator and pantry, because they don't have the judgment to make good choices about what foods to eat, when to eat, or how much. Giving free choice to youngsters often means they won't be hungry enough to eat nutritious meals and snacks.

FIVE: *Teach Your Young Child Good Eating Behavior – Such As Staying At The Table When Eating*

Work out what rules you want during eating and begin to teach them to your children. Children don"t automatically sit long enough to eat unless you teach them to. Plan reasonable consequences – not just threats. Children should also be expected to sit for only short times at meals. Young preschoolers might sit for 10 minutes and older preschoolers and kindergartners for 20 minutes.

SIX: *Eat With Your Children As Much As Possible*

Sit with them, facing them, and actually eat, communicating and socializing with them as you dine. Don't do other things like talking on the phone, working on your computer, or watching TV while eating with your child.

SEVEN: *Sensible Strategies Can Motivate Young Children To Eat Better*

Children need to be hungry when you serve healthy meals and snacks. It's best if they don't eat for at least two hours before the next planned meal or snack. If your child is "starving" before dinner, give her some raw vegetables to eat. They're healthy and not as filling as crackers, cheese, etc. and she'll probably be more willing to eat them at that time. Portion sizes at the meal should not be so large that they seem impossible for a young child to finish. Try to make sure the child is hungry, comfortably seated (no dangling feet!), not eating alone, and included in the conversation.

• GUIDELINES FOR TEACHING YOUNG CHILDREN ABOUT HEALTHY EATING •

EIGHT: *For Light Or Picky Eaters, Limit Milk And Forget About Juice*
The guideline for preschoolers and kindergartners is approximately 16 to 24 ounces of milk (including cheese and yogurt), no juice, and unlimited water. Too much milk will decrease children's appetites for all the other nutritious food they need. Record your child's liquid intake for three consecutive days to get an accurate picture, not just your best estimate, of his consumption of milk and juice. Juice is no longer considered quality nutrition and should be eliminated or, at most, be limited to 4 to 6 ounces daily of 100% fruit juice. (Sodas and sports drinks are not recommended for young children to drink.)

NINE: *Combat Picky Eating By Cutting Back On Sweet, Fatty, And Salty Snacks*
Letting children fill up on sweet foods like sugary cereals and desserts and salty and/or fatty foods like chicken nuggets, French fries, macaroni and cheese, or potato chips can increase pickiness. A diet too high in these foods makes healthier foods (chicken, broccoli, carrots, strawberries, apricots, whole wheat breads, cereals) seem tasteless—and therefore not worth eating. Try also keeping three-day food logs to look at your child's nutrition and calories more objectively.

TEN: *Have Your Child Help With Growing Food And Preparing It*
Most children love planting gardens and delight in cooking with their parents. Children feel connected, engaged, and emotionally close to their parents when gardening and preparing meals together. Both activities have an added bonus for a picky eater who can have a chance to get familiar with a wider range of foods.

ELEVEN: *Children Overeat For A Variety Of Reasons*
Keeping a short-term food and drink log can be helpful here, too. Parents need to assess why eating is such an important activity for their child. Looking at the healthy balance of the food served and what foods are available at other times is essential. *Do you need to learn more about nutrition?* • *Is eating too much of a frequent activity in your home?* • *Is there too much unhealthy food in the house?* • *How much exercise is the family getting? You can log that too for a few weeks.* • *How are your child's emotional needs being fulfilled?* • *Is there enough cuddling?* • *Do you spend enjoyable and meaningful time with your child?* • *Does your family spend too much time in front of the TV, and even eat while watching TV?* • *Does your child have other children to play with?* • *Do you know how to get your child's cooperation with your rules and limits?* Stress can come from any of these areas, or from parents' not knowing how to get their young child's cooperation, resulting in lots of yelling, threatening, and punishing. Too much stress in the home can lead to a child's overeating in order to relax.

TWELVE: *Exercise Should Be A Part Of Your Family's Daily Life*
Everyone needs exercise. Many children and their parents need more than they're getting. Spend some time figuring out what you can do to build the attitude that daily physical activity as a family (and individually) is essential and enjoyable.

B. ANNYE ROTHENBERG, Ph.D., *author*, has been a child/parent psychologist and a specialist in child rearing and development of young children for more than 25 years. Her parenting psychology practice is in Emerald Hills, California. She is also an adjunct clinical assistant professor of pediatrics at Stanford University School of Medicine and frequently consults to pediatricians and teachers. Dr. Rothenberg was the founder/director of the Child Rearing parenting program in Palo Alto, California, and is the author of the award-winning book *Parentmaking* and other parenting education books for parenting guidance professionals. Her first two books in this series are *Mommy and Daddy Are Always Supposed to Say Yes … Aren't They?* (2007) and *Why Do I Have To?* (2008). She is the mother of one son.

DAVID T. WENZEL, *illustrator*, has been creating children's books for over 25 years. His work covers a vast area of subject matter, and he has gained recognition for visualizing the fantastic creatures in J.R.R. Tolkien's **The Hobbit** and the carefree adventures of **Rudolph The Red Nosed Reindeer**. Other titles include Max Lucado's **A Hat for Ivan**, Eileen Spinelli's **Baby Loves You So Much** and Annye Rothenberg's **Why Do I Have To?**, plus many more. David works in watercolor or colored inks on Waterford watercolor paper. He is married, has two sons, and lives in Connecticut.

ACKNOWLEDGEMENTS

The author is very grateful to *SuAnn and Kevin Kiser* for their outstanding critiques and collaboration on the Children's Story, and to *Caroline Grannan* for her excellent editing of the Parents' Manual. *Cathleen O'Brien* has done a wonderful job on book design. Thanks to *Detta Penna* for her good work in designing the nutrition tables. Many thanks to pediatric dietitians *Judith Levine, M.S., R.D.; JoAnn Hattner, M.P.H.,R.D.*; and *Anne Kolker, M.S., R.D.*, for their valuable reviews of the information in this book. The feedback provided by the parents in focus groups from *Ladera Community Church Preschool* in Portola Valley and *Merry Moppets Preschool* in Belmont, both in California, was also very helpful. We are very appreciative of the thorough reviews and thoughtful suggestions made by the following pediatricians: *Harry Dennis, M.D., Palo Alto Medical Foundation (Palo Alto site); Annette Hwang, M.D.* and *Jelena Vukicevic, M.D.,* both from *Welch Road Pediatric Medical Group, Palo Alto;* and *Mary Ann Zetes, M.D., Altos Pediatric Associates, Los Altos,* all in California.

"*This is a book that parents will find invaluable in dealing with a common parenting struggle – encouraging healthy eating habits.* By giving parents practical nutritional advice (and educating young children about the difference between treats and healthy foods), Dr. Rothenberg provides the tools to foster healthy relationships with food. Being the mother of a picky eater, I have already put her tips to practical use, and they work! I will definitely recommend this book to all my patients struggling to provide their children with a balanced diet."

—Suzanne M. Einsiedl, RN, MSN; Pediatric Nurse Practitioner and mother of three (ages 6, 8 and 10)

"Dr. Rothenberg's easy-to-read book on healthy eating for young children provides the framework for lifelong healthy eating habits. The parents' guidance section makes this a book for the entire family. *It offers great nutritional, behavioral, and social reminders that make this book a must-read.*"

—Lisa and Rick Deming, parents of a 6-year-old girl

"*I love the concept of this book – a wonderful, engaging story for kids, as well as a thoroughly researched manual for parents about teaching children healthy eating habits.* It isn't just a book filled with statistics; it has charming, colorful illustrations and lots of useful strategies for parents. Dr. Rothenberg has clearly done her homework, and I will be confident in recommending this book to our many patrons who are clamoring for information on this very subject."

—Jill Ehrhorn, Senior Librarian, Palo Alto (CA) Children's Library

"*Please, give me some advice that will work!* This is a common plea from parents struggling with heated issues around eating. They'll be relieved to **read this outstanding book with its developmentally appropriate advice**. And the engaging story for young children effectively teaches the key messages about healthy eating. Our school has glowing praise for Dr. Rothenberg's real and workable techniques for concerned families."

—Susan Kelly, Director, St. Paul's Nursery School, Burlingame, CA

"I love the unique combination of a story for children combined with a guide for parents in Dr. Rothenberg's newest book, *I Like To Eat Treats.* It encourages collaboration between the young child and parent in the quest for improving children's eating habits and gives parents the credible, accurate nutrition information needed to answer their children's questions. **This is a great way to teach young children about healthier eating.**"

—Judith Levine, MS, RD; Nutritionist and author of *Helping Your Child Lose Weight the Healthy Way*

"Dr. Rothenberg's latest book puts nutrition in language young children can easily understand, helping them develop good eating habits at an early age. The book also provides guidance and solutions to many issues that parents run into while trying to form healthy family eating habits. *I highly recommend this book to parents with young children.*"

—Thomas Kwan, parent of a 6-year-old boy

"Dr. Rothenberg has created yet another wonderfully helpful story for parents, teachers, and grandparents alike! *For those of us who want to encourage healthy eating habits while explaining the facts about good nutrition in a kid-friendly way, this book is invaluable.* Thank you, Annye, for helping parents and teachers with this important task!"

—Linda Westcott, Co-Director, University Heights Montessori School, Menlo Park, CA; and grandmother of 10

"*Annye Rothenberg's book is an essential and wonderful guide* to get us, the grownups, on track in realizing it is our responsibility to teach our children all the essentials of eating well."

—Jesse Ziff Cool, founder of several healthful eating establishments on the San Francisco Peninsula, including the Cool Café at Stanford University, and author of several books, including *Simply Organic*

"Dr. Rothenberg has done it again, this time applying her practical advice and humor to the topic of childhood nutrition. *The engaging children's story has made an important impact on our children's understanding of what healthy foods are.* And the golden nuggets in the parents' section have helped us navigate the difficult, and often emotional, journey of really teaching healthy eating habits, polite table manners, and lifelong exercise routines. *Using these techniques has brought joy back into our family mealtimes and our parenting.*"

—Ramón and Cynthia Olavarría, parents of four children (ages 6, 4½, 2½ and 10 months)

"*Annye Rothenberg is a master at equipping parents with a pathway to making healthy eating a fun, whole-family experience.*"

—Jamie Holden, Director, Trinity Presbyterian Nursery School, and Parent Educator, San Carlos, CA

"*At last, a concise, authoritative guide to help parents and children navigate a healthy path through the confusing world of nutrition.* This third book in her series fills an important need by providing parents with principles, facts, practical examples, and parenting guidelines to address the challenging issues of healthy eating and healthy weight. It is uniquely helpful because Dr. Rothenberg teaches parents age-appropriate expectations and links those with the tools to use when coping with the many common food issues such as introducing new foods, mealtime rules, and dealing with cupboard-raiding. And the brightly illustrated children's story provides parents with a winning strategy that will engage their young children as active participants in healthy decision-making."

—Mary Ann Carmack, MD, PhD; Chair, Department of Pediatrics, Palo Alto (CA) Medical Foundation

Be sure to read Dr. Annye Rothenberg's other All-In-One Books.

Mommy and Daddy Are Always Supposed to Say Yes...Aren't They?

A STORY FOR CHILDREN—Alex gets mad when he doesn't get his way. Like many preschoolers, he insists that his parents should always let him have what he wants. Right now. Or else. Through a series of everyday events, Alex starts to understand that maybe this isn't always a good idea. When he plays the parent in a fun role reversal, he begins to see things differently. Alex learns that even when Mom and Dad say no, they still love him ... a lot. The story and its witty, warm, and expressive illustrations teach children a lesson that parents want them to learn.   **WITH A PARENT MANUAL**—Parents need help reinforcing these lessons. What are the secrets to building your preschool children's self-esteem without turning them into little royalty? What's going on in their minds, and why don't they get the message about who's the parent? What rules do you need, and how do you deal realistically with the differences between your parenting and your spouse's? The guide includes all this and more, to build your understanding and skills.

*"This is one book that could change your life. This unique children's story and the parents' guide teach a strong, respectful approach that is neither too permissive nor too controlling. **Preschoolers will thrive with this kind of direction from the adults in their lives—and everyone will be the happier for it."***
— Alan Greene, MD, Pediatrician; Clinical Faculty, Stanford University School of Medicine; founder of www.DrGreene.com.

Why Do I Have To?

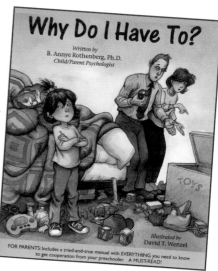

A STORY FOR CHILDREN—Sophie wonders why there are so many rules and why her parents want her to follow them. Through the day's experiences, she starts to understand why parents have rules—and then Sophie comes up with her own delightful rule. This story, with its warm, funny, and endearing illustrations, teaches your preschoolers just what you want them to learn.   **WITH A PARENT MANUAL**—Provides the keys to how preschoolers think so parents can understand why they behave the way they do. It helps you use respectful, age-appropriate approaches that make it easier for your children to do what's asked, and teaches new and more effective consequences. ***This manual clears up much of the conflicting advice that parents hear.*** Its concise and practical information puts parents on a confident path toward the outcomes we all desire for our children.

*"**Annye Rothenberg again demonstrates a keen understanding of a child's motivation** – this time, how hard it is for little ones to obey rules they may not understand. In a simple story, she creates everyday situations that challenge the patience of a precocious preschooler, yet ultimately demonstrate the importance of setting limits in a thoughtful, loving way. **Like Mommy and Daddy Are Always Supposed to Say Yes … Aren't They?**, Rothenberg's latest children's book is paired with a useful parents' manual that gives insightful techniques to help children understand rules and limits. **Her books are some of the closest things to a User's Manual for parents out there!"***
—Peggy Spear, Editor, Bay Area Parent Magazine

To order these books: visit www.PerfectingParentingPress.com where you can order online or call (810) 388-9500 or fax (810) 388-9502 or mail to 35 Ash Drive, Kimball, MI 48074. Also available at www.amazon.com.

And look for Dr. Rothenberg's fourth book in this series for preschoolers and their parents,
I Don't Want To Go To The Toilet, available in 2011.